Also by Tom Jackson

Tom Jackson's POWER LETTER EXPRESS

Tom Jackson and Bill Buckingham

TIMES BOOKS

RANDOM HOUSE

Library of Congress Cataloging-in-Publication Data

Jackson, Tom.
    [Power letter express]
    Tom Jackson's power letter express / Tom Jackson and Bill
Buckingham.—1st ed.
        p.   cm.
    ISBN 0–8129–2131–3
    1. Cover letters. 2. Applications for positions. I. Buckingham,
Bill. II. Title.
    HF5383.J263   1994
    808'.06665—dc20   94–12857

Manufactured in the United States of America
9 8 7 6 5 4 3 2
First Edition
Design by ROBERT BULL DESIGN

CONTENTS

Dear Job Seeker,

We know how important powerful letters will be in your successful job search.

The first impression a prospective employer will have about you will probably come from the cover letter that accompanies your resume. This initial communication can generate interest and attention that will carry all the way through to the interview and offer, or it can turn off the reader even before he or she gets to your resume.

Think about it: the resume is a carefully sculpted advertisement—often with multiple copies prepared for a general readership. The cover letter, or any letter that is not a form letter, is written communication between you and a specific person. Before your first physical contact all you are to the reader is a set of words on paper. It is no exaggeration to say that your ability to write a cover letter is essential in generating the job offers you want. This book addresses that issue.

This book shows you how to write letters to employers that will greatly increase your chance of getting the job offers you want, and even accomplish other job search business. We call these powerful letters, appropriately enough, "power letters."

We provide examples of power letters that you can easily use in many situations—from "prepping" an employer before a job interview to delaying an offer in hopes of a higher offer from someone else to protecting your current job while answering a "blind ad." And many, many more based on the authors' three decades of combined experience and the advice of scores of employment experts.

Follow the easy steps to your own most powerful letters.

Best of luck,

Tom Jackson and Bill Buckingham

ONE

POWERFUL
COVER
LETTERS

The medium of the job search is language: we ask, we assert, we request, we write, we interview and we negotiate. How powerful the language is depends on how well we communicate. The people with the most successful job search are most frequently those who do the best job of communicating—clearly, forcefully and convincingly. Since many of the earlier stages of the job search are conducted by mail, it has become increasingly clear that to win in the competitive career marketplace, a person must master the art of letter writing. In this chapter, we'll introduce the power letter and show you how to write one to accompany your resume.

WHAT IS A POWER LETTER?

A power letter is designed to produce a desired action or outcome. You write a power cover letter, for example, not to say simply, "Here is my resume." You write it in a way that will get the employer to read your resume with the option of an interview very much in mind. It tells a story that encourages further attention to the resume.

The power letter follows a specific format: it is composed of four sections or paragraphs, which are presented in a particular order. Each paragraph serves a different function. This format can be applied to any kind of letter, no matter what your goal.

THE FOUR COMPONENTS
OF A POWER LETTER

1. OPENING: DEMANDING ATTENTION

The opening paragraph of the power letter captures the reader's attention, signaling that you are prepared to communicate something relevant. It is not simply a form letter. A power cover letter contains information that connects you to the employer—perhaps facts about the company's market situation, the products or services the company provides, particular challenges or opportunities the company or its industry faces. It might refer to a mutual friend.

FOR EXAMPLE:

> Dear Mr. Durkovic,
> I understand that Aspect Corporation is one of the few final contenders for the major Internet Security Protocol contract to be awarded by the U.S. Defense Department. As one of the early designers of the original specifications, I felt it useful to contact you.

2. PROPOSITION: DESCRIBING A BENEFIT

The second paragraph of the power letter makes a positive proposition: a statement of potential benefit that could accrue to the reader or the company she or he represents. This could reflect solutions offered, value you will add, or opportunities that you can meet. It answers the question: Why should I hire you?

FOR EXAMPLE:

> Given my knowledge of this technology, I believe that I could contribute great value as a member of your project team. I am writing to request an interview to discuss this.

3. COMPELLING CASE:
SUPPORTING THE PROPOSITION

The third paragraph of the power letter provides compelling evidence that supports your proposition. It directs the reader's attention to those sections of the resume that will convince the employer that you can do what you say you will do in the power proposition.

FOR EXAMPLE:

> As you can see from my resume, from 1989 to late last year I was a leader in Contracam Engineering's encryption section. There we did much of the original thinking for a very exciting new methodology. I left the company when they relocated to Rhinebeck, New York, and am now considering joining an organization where I can continue this important research.

4. CLOSING: SETTING UP THE NEXT STEP

The closing paragraph of the power letter sets up the next action that will move to produce the result you intended. A power letter ends with your proposing the next move: you'll call the employer soon, say within a week, if you do not hear from him. Keep the initiative in your hands, ensuring that you have another communication with the employer and increasing your chances of getting the job interview.

FOR EXAMPLE:

> I look forward to an opportunity to meet with you and your colleagues and will call your office early next week to set up a time to meet.

BEFORE AND AFTER:
CONVERTING A WEAK COVER LETTER INTO A POWER LETTER

Now that you know the four sections of a power letter and the function each serves, follow our thinking as we transform a weak cover letter into a power letter.

Consider the paragraphs below from weak letters. As you read each one, can you see what makes it weak? After each of the weak paragraphs, we give our criticism and rewrite suggestions.

WEAK OPENING PARAGRAPH

> To Whom It May Concern,
> According to the ad in Sunday's <u>Register</u>, you need a project manager for your plant. I am sending my resume for your perusal.

Critique: The opening fails to attract the reader's attention. It is not addressed to a specific person, it states the obvious, it uses a tired, formal phrase, "for your perusal," and it contains nothing about the company or industry that could connect the job seeker to the employer.

REWRITE: THE POWER OPENING

> Dear Mr. Avery,
> I was extremely impressed by Kensico Plant's recent Rondout Creek cleanup effort. As a deeply committed environmentalist, I believe I can be a valuable contributing member of your project team.

POWER POINTS

- **Address a real person.**
- **Give concrete knowledge of something the company is doing.**
- **Link the job seeker to the concerns of the company.**
- **Go beyond the help-wanted advertisement—indicating that additional research was done.**

WEAK SECOND PARAGRAPH

> I have done project work before and found it interesting. I am looking for an opportunity to build a stable future, and hope your firm could be the place.

Critique: This contains no attractive proposition for the employer. It does not suggest how hiring the candidate will benefit the company. The focus is on the writer's need.

REWRITE: THE POWER PROPOSITION

> I believe the qualities you need closely match ones I've developed as a seasoned environmental planner with one of the largest food processors in the Northeast. In my ten years of focusing on environmental concerns, I've developed ways to use available technology in an innovative and practical way. I believe I can help you meet your current challenges and those that arise in the future.

POWER POINTS

- **Show thinking about the problem.**
- **Cite similar experience over time.**
- **Commit to reaching goals.**
- **Stress practical rewards.**

WEAK THIRD PARAGRAPH

> I am sure that after reading my resume you will agree that I have the right qualifications for the job.

Critique: This paragraph assumes that the employer will get all the information he needs from the resume; it does not provide specifics; it shows arrogance, not confidence, and little knowledge of the employer's situation.

Rewrite: The Power Case

As you will see from my attached resume, in my last three years at the Maverick Corporation, I developed a highly successful set of new measurement standards, which allowed the company to anticipate many potential difficulties and head off problems. We were also praised for our ability to respond to emergencies and get cooperation from local media and government. We saved money and built up a good reputation.

Power Points

- **Give specifics.**
- **Stress new approaches.**
- **Demonstrate financial benefits.**
- **Show confidence in self and results.**

Weak Closing

I am looking forward to meeting with you to discuss this challenging position in more detail. You can reach me at the number on my resume if you would like to arrange an interview.

Critique: Does not provoke action, or give sense of importance.

Rewrite: The Power Closing

I know that my capabilities could be of value to you and your company, and I think it would be useful to meet to discuss them. I will contact you or your office on March 30th to arrange a meeting. If you have any preliminary questions after you have read my resume, please call.

Power Points

- **Recap benefit.**
- **Suggest next step.**
- **Take responsibility for next action.**
- **Be specific about action and date.**

POWER LETTER REVIEW

Answer the following questions:

What differentiates a power letter from a regular letter?

What does a power opening do?

What is a proposition—the second paragraph of the power letter?

What is the purpose of the compelling case?

What do you want to accomplish with a good close?

POWER LETTER WARM-UP

Read the following letters—some are very poor, others not so bad—and see how you would make them more powerful if you were this person's career counselor. Check each of them against the power points shown below:

POWER POINTS FOR POWER LETTERS

- Address to a real person.
- Give concrete knowledge of something the company is doing.
- Link the job seeker to the concerns of the company.
- Go beyond the help-wanted advertisement, indicating that additional research was done.
- Show thinking about the problem.
- Cite similar experience over time.
- Commit to reaching goals.
- Stress practical rewards.
- Give specifics.
- Stress new approaches.
- Demonstrate financial benefits.
- Show confidence in self and results.
- Recap benefit.
- Suggest next step.
- Take responsibility for next action.
- Be specific about action and date.

To whom it may concern,

I seek a position with MicroWare, and in return I offer over one and a half year's experience as an administrative manager of Electronics Boutique, "The Home Computer Store."

While with Electronics Boutique, I have had a major impact on the store's success. Sales are up over thirty percent from last year. The store's standing has leaped from 106th in the chain to 55th and has also received two nearly perfect district manager inspections. It has won seven of the last eleven "Store of the Month" awards, out of fifteen competing stores.

As an experienced administrative manager, I have increased store sales and efficiency through my persistent attention to detail. My excellent communication skills have also been vital in increasing the sales efficiency of my employees as well as greatly increasing the store's customer base. I am very knowledgeable about personal computers and the software that runs them.

If hired, I would bring my detailed computer knowledge and my proven skills to track and control inventory, and I would improve the efficiency of my co-workers. I would be happy to meet with you for an interview. Please feel free to call me anytime. My number is (914) 555-1224. I am currently earning $20,000.

Sincerely,

Hello:

Your classified ad in the <u>Sunday Journal</u> for a marketing manager prompts this response. I am well organized, detailed-oriented and have good marketing, sales and public relation skills.

For the past three and a half years I successfully obtained press coverage for MicroTech Learning Systems and for its products (video-based training for IBM PC computers) in many newspapers and magazines (and not just in trade publications), and directed sales efforts that brought in a million dollars in revenues. I was also responsible for editing the company's newsletter and for programming our catalog on disk.

My resume is enclosed for your review. I look forward to a face-to-face opportunity to discuss the many valuable contributions I could make to your organization's marketing efforts. Hoping to hear from you soon, I remain,

Cordially yours,

Dear MicroWare:

I read your recent ad for the office management position in the Sunday Journal with interest and would like to learn more about the job and your company.

For the past fourteen years, I have been working in public relations, development, and editorial. I am a detailed-oriented, highly organized professional, able to work independently, and am adept at initiating and completing assorted, simultaneous projects. Much of my experience involves writing, editing, producing publications, brochures, grant applications, news releases, speeches, and direct mail projects, as well as creating and coordinating details for special events, and designing and placing advertising. I think my organizational, public relations and editing skills match the requirements outlined in your ad description.

I intend to make the transition from public relations to another area of administrative work and am particularly interested in information systems and publishing. I also want to leave the nonprofit realm and join a commercial establishment.

If you feel my education and administrative experience fit this position, please contact me at 914-555-4545, ext. 112.

Thank you for your time and consideration.

Sincerely,

TWO

DRAFTING YOUR OWN POWERFUL COVER LETTERS

PURPOSE OF THE COVER LETTER

The purpose of the cover letter is to get a reader to pay particular attention to your resume and request for an interview—to customize the communication beyond the printed form and create interest in meeting you.

It is time to get started on your own next cover letter. Writing this assumes that you have already prepared your resume, are clear about your job target, and are ready to send it to a particular employer.

If you are not actively searching for a job but anticipate doing so soon, pretend you are after a real job and use this hands-on learning tool to prepare your next letter.

In this first draft, you can try different ideas to see how they sound. Experiment with the language and an assertive style. There is no need to get the writing right the first time. Whatever you say at this stage can be revised later. For help on possible paragraphs see Chapter 9 on page 58.

POWER LETTER DRAFTING FORM I

Answer the following questions:

PRELIMINARY

1. What is the title of the job you seek?

_____

2. Identity:

Name the company to which you are writing:

_____

The person with whom you want to communicate and his or her title:

_____

_____

Address:

_____

_____

Phone: _____

3. What do you know about the company's needs, concerns, desires?

_____

_____

_____

_____

_____

_____

THE OPENING

Draft a power opening, two or three lines that will connect you to the
employer and interest her in seeing you:

Dear _____ :

_____

_____

_____

_____

THE PROPOSITION

Draft a statement declaring the direct benefit(s) you offer to the employer.

_____

_____

_____

_____

_____

_____

_____

_____

THE COMPELLING CASE

Draft a compelling case—what you have done in the past that demonstrates or lends credence to the above proposition. Refer to your resume in writing this section. How can you enhance your resume's relevance to the employer's needs?

_____

_____

_____

_____

_____

_____

_____

_____

THE CLOSE

Draft your power closing: state the next action you will take to increase the possibility of a meeting.

_____

_____

_____

_____

You can use the space on page 15 to make a second draft of this letter. If you are ready to put this letter into final form, go to Chapter 3 for ideas on how to polish it. Alternatively, you might want to use the following pages to draft one or two additional letters before making a final draft of any of them.

Power Letter 1: Second Draft

Use this form or type on a word processor.

_____(Addressee's name and title)

_____(Company)

_____(Address)

_____(City, state and zip)

Dear _____:

_____

_____

_____

_____

_____

_____

_____

_____

_____

_____

_____

_____

_____

_____

_____

_____

_____

_____

_____

_____

_____

_____

_____

_____

Answer the following questions:

PRELIMINARY

1. What is the title of the job you seek?

_____

2. Identity:

Name the company to which you are writing:

_____

The person to whom you are writing and his or her title:

_____

_____

Address:

_____

_____

Phone: _____

3. What do you know about the company's needs, concerns, desires?

_____

_____

_____

_____

_____

THE OPENING

Draft a power opening: two or three lines that will connect you to the
employer and interest her in seeing you:

Dear _____ :

_____

_____

__ _____

_____

THE PROPOSITION

Draft a statement declaring the direct benefit(s) you offer to the employer.

_____

_____

_____

_____

THE COMPELLING CASE

Draft a compelling case—what you have done in the past that demonstrates or lends credence to the above proposition. Refer to your resume in this section. How can you enhance the resume's relevance to the employer's needs?

_____

_____

_____

_____

THE CLOSE

Draft your power closing: state the next action you will take to increase the possibility of a meeting.

_____

_____

_____

_____

You can use the space on page 18 to make a second draft of this letter. If you are ready to put this letter into final form, go to Chapter 3 for ideas on how to polish it. Alternatively, you might want to use the following pages to draft one or two additional letters before making a final draft of any of them.

POWER LETTER 2: SECOND DRAFT

Use this form or type on a word processor.

_____ (Addressee's name and title)

_____ (Company)

_____ (Address)

_____ (City, state and zip)

Dear _____:

_____

_____

_____

_____

_____

_____

_____

_____

_____

_____

_____

_____

_____

_____

_____

_____

_____

_____

_____

_____

_____

_____

_____

_____

POWER LETTER DRAFTING FORM 3

Answer the following questions:

PRELIMINARY

1. What is the title of the job you seek?

_____

2. Identity:
Name the company to which you are writing:

_____

The person to whom you are writing and his or her title:

_____

_____

Address:

_____

_____

_____

Phone: _____

3. What do you know about the company's needs, concerns, desires?

_____

_____

_____

_____

_____

_____

_____

_____

_____

_____

_____

_____

THE OPENING

Draft a power opening: two or three lines that will connect you to the employer and interest her in seeing you:

Dear _____ :

_____

_____

_____

THE PROPOSITION

Draft a statement declaring the direct benefit(s) you offer the employer.

_____

_____

_____

THE COMPELLING CASE

Draft a compelling case—what you have done in the past that demonstrates or lends credence to the above proposition. Refer to your resume in writing this section. How can you enhance the relevance of the resume to the employer's needs?

_____

_____

_____

THE CLOSE

Draft your power closing: state the next action you will take to increase the possibility of a meeting.

_____

_____

_____

You can use the space on page 21 to make a second draft of this letter. If you are ready to put this letter into final form, go to Chapter 3 for ideas on how to polish it. Alternatively, you might want to use the following pages to draft one or two additional letters before making a final draft of any of them.

POWER LETTER 3: SECOND DRAFT

Use this form, or type on a word processor.

_____ (Addressee's name and title)

_____ (Company)

_____ (Address)

_____ (City, state and zip)

Dear _____:

_____

_____

_____

_____

_____

_____

_____

_____

_____

_____

_____

_____

_____

_____

_____

_____

_____

_____

_____

_____

_____

_____

_____

THREE

POLISHING
YOUR
COVER LETTERS

Your first draft allows you to try out your thinking. When you have finished the letter, edit or rewrite it to ensure each paragraph flows smoothly into the next. You should make a couple of passes on it.

DO'S AND DON'TS

Here are some do's and don'ts to consider as you edit your power paragraphs.

DO

- Keep in mind that less (verbiage) is more (powerful) when writing a power letter. Choose your words carefully, eliminate archaic language and overly formal styles, use action verbs and the active voice ("I built a new order processing department" rather than "A new order processing department was built").
- Use the proper terms to convey technical abilities and expertise. If you don't know the "insider" language, read up in the appropriate trade journals, newsletters, and magazines. (See Chapter 10 on how to find these publications.)
- Keep the tone of your power letter professional: enthusiastic, assertive, and right to the point.

DON'TS

- Don't try to achieve perfection in your first draft. Plan on several drafts or rewrites to come up with just the right tone. Once you have assembled the final paragraphs you can edit further for appearance and layout.
- Don't put on your editor's cap until you've finished at least one full draft of your letter. The "writer" and the "critic" functions are different and often are in conflict. So first compose a whole draft using the forms above, and then sit back and correct what you've written.

POWER COMPONENTS QUALITY CHECKLIST

CONTENT

- In your opening paragraph, have you shown knowledge of the company, connected yourself to an opportunity, or otherwise demanded the attention of the employer?
- In your second paragraph, would an employer understand the potential benefits you offer? Have you painted a clear picture of the value you add?
- In your third paragraph, have you made a compelling case for your value proposition? Have you demonstrated from your past experience that you'll be able to provide the benefits you've offered to the employer? Does your resume bear this out?
- In your closing paragraph, have you clearly spelled out when you will make contact and how?

WRITING STYLE

- Are the sentences and paragraphs in your letters short and to the point? (The letter should not exceed one page—with one-inch margins.)
- Do you use strong action words (for example, designed, organized, re-engineered) to begin each statement that describes your capabilities and accomplishments?
- Are all the claims in your power letters easy to understand?
- Have you repeated any information in your power letters that you could consolidate?
- Did you use an active (rather than passive) voice?
- Did you triple-check for errors in spelling, grammar, punctuation?
- Did you have someone else review it?

QUALITY APPEARANCE

A letter that looks weak on the page may not get read, no matter what you have to say or how well you say it. After you're satisfied with the content of your power cover letters, turn your attention to their layout and appearance.

Business communications should be typed on a good quality typewriter or, more preferably, entered in a word processor and laser printed. Word-processing programs allow you to customize your power letters for particular employers and to minimize the chance of errors in grammar, punctuation, and spelling.

Word processing software and laser printers let you experiment with different layouts, type sizes, and fonts to find the most readable and professional presentation.

If you have a choice of fonts, select a classic serif typeface (such as Times Roman). Stay away from novelty fonts or script that imitates handwriting.

Keep the look of your power letters simple. Make the margins at least one inch wide all around. Use one-line spacing between sentences within a paragraph (single spacing) and two lines between each paragraph (double spacing). Don't indent the paragraphs: use the most accepted format, which is the "block format," shown in the sample power letters in Chapter 11.

If you do not have a computer or word processor at home or in your office, you can usually get access to one through libraries, counseling centers, colleges, or copy shops. If you don't type, have someone prepare your final draft on a computer and print it out on a laser or ink-jet printer. Do not use outdated dot matrix printers.

When printing, use a high quality paper stock, usually bond paper of at least twenty-pound weight. Do not use colored paper. Choose white, ivory, buff, or off-white.

Send your letter and resume in an envelope that matches your letter. If you are sending several pages—i.e., cover letter, resume or other documents—consider using a 9 x 12-inch flat envelope.

APPEARANCE CHECKLIST

- **Does your power letter fit neatly on one page?**
- **Is the layout simple, professional, attractive, and easy to read?**
- **Are the margins at the sides and bottom at least one inch wide?**
- **Is the letter single spaced with double spacing between paragraphs?**

ATTENTION COMPUTER USERS!

Power Letter Express for IBM PC and compatibles is the easiest way to write a strategic cover letter, interview follow-up letters, and a host of other job-related letters. Nine out of ten job seekers are knocked out of the screening process because they don't know how to write words, phrases, and paragraphs to personalize their letters effectively. This easy-to-use software program creates winning letters in a matter of minutes. A Targeted Employer Database is built in to maintain and let you update your lists of prospective employers. Available from Permax Systems, Inc., for $29.95: (800) 233-6460.

FOUR

OVERCOMING OBSTACLES

Many job seekers have (or believe they have) special obstacles to overcome in their job search. They may have been out of the workforce for many years, or have a physical handicap, or lack the so-called minimum educational requirements for a job they know they can do well. In this chapter, we show sample paragraphs from cover letters that successfully address many potential obstacles to getting the job interview.

POWER LETTERS FOR SPECIAL SITUATIONS

1. YOU HAVE BEEN ABSENT FROM THE TRADITIONAL WORKFORCE FOR SEVERAL YEARS.

This includes people who have been rearing children, retirees who want to re-enter the workforce, and those self-employed who have decided, after a good try at solo employment, to "go on staff."

It is especially important to find out in advance what each employer you expect to contact is looking for and then to describe in detail the specific skills you offer in your power proposition.

When you make your compelling case, use whatever benefits of your nontraditional work life you can to support your proposition. If you have no direct experience in the job itself, emphasize related skills and education. Don't apologize.

In my time as a homemaker, I have developed a strong sense of the importance of the small details that take customer service from a concept to a working reality. I can teach this to others.

I know the job requires a person with very good computer skills, not just word processing. In the past two years, I have honed my computer skills to a high degree, and I am familiar with most of the products of Lotus, Microsoft and the various Apple platforms. Being away from the regular job market has allowed me to practice and learn more than I could have on a full-time job.

Being self-employed for three years taught me many invaluable lessons that could assist you in your plan to "re-engineer" your operations. I have had to make the best use of systems and to build in every efficiency. I believe that my output per week is triple what it would have been in a more traditional setting. I know I can translate this hands-on experience to your six offices and help you make your business far more efficient.

2. YOU DO NOT MEET THE DESIRED EDUCATIONAL LEVELS.

In a strong buyers' market—more people than jobs—companies often set unreasonably high education requirements—asking for a four-year degree when less would suffice. If you are finding that you are not meeting the requested levels, you might frame your situation as follows:

> I know you are looking for someone with an M.S. in economics. This is a valid requirement; however, I believe that I am an exception to the rule. For six years I worked in the financial markets with some of the top deal makers in the business. What I have learned in that time about the practical side of the business has exceeded what I would have learned in any school, and you will benefit from this.

3. YOU DO NOT HAVE ENOUGH RELEVANT EXPERIENCE.

Your work experience has been in another field. In this situation, emphasize the most relevant personal qualities and skills, as shown in the following:

> I know you are seeking someone with several years experience in market research. However, even though most of my experience was in data processing, I believe my approach to the job will be strengthened by this. Given the need for new ways to interpret consumer preferences, my approach—which would be based in modeling—could be more imaginative than someone with years of marketing experience. I am looking forward to the opportunity to elaborate on this further in a meeting with you.

4. YOU HAVE BEEN LAID OFF.

You lost your most recent job as a result of a layoff. Try a power paragraph like the following:

> I'm one of many people who've been laid off from X company in the last few months due to the severe downsizing that has affected our entire industry. This separation was in no way related to my competence, and my personal referrals will clearly demonstrate my successes in the job.

If your resume can be written in such a way that a job loss is not flagged, as illustrated in the resume section on page 74, then you may wish to leave it out of the cover letter and discuss it during the interview.

5. YOU ARE APPLYING FOR A POSITION THAT IS A STEP DOWN.

You were laid off some time ago and are applying for a job that is a step down from your previous job—and for which you're probably overqualified. Include something like the following in your letter:

> I have more experience and depth than appears called for in the position you have advertised. If the position is narrow in scope and unchangeable, this might be a disadvantage. On the other hand, because of my extensive background in regulatory matters, I can take on more of the legal burden in the job and you will realize some savings. I have no problem with the stated compensation and know that over time, as our relationship strengthens and I demonstrate superior results, the investment will pay off.

6. YOU ARE AN OLDER WORKER.

If you fear that an employer might pass you over for a younger candidate, don't telegraph your age in the letter. Screen the dates in your resume by using a functional resume format (see Chapter 6, page 40). If after an interview you still feel the employer is discriminating against you because of your age, write a post-interview power letter that addresses this situation.

> I was very excited to hear the challenges that you spelled out in your description of the department's long-range goals. I know that my extensive experience—three decades worth—will be a big plus given the range of possibilities that will arise. I believe this is a situation where depth is required, and I have that depth.

7. You are a young worker.

You are afraid the potential employer is looking for someone more seasoned, the "screening" procedure just described for the older worker. If you think it is to your advantage to point out your age, however, you could include a paragraph like this:

> I believe the fact that I am just entering the field from college is very much to my advantage. Committed to making a mark in this industry, I am a fast learner and willing to look at things in fresh ways. I am confident there are very few problems I can't solve in collaboration with others on the team.

8. You are planning to relocate.

If you are searching for a job in a distant city, and are willing to pay for your relocation, but are worried that potential employers might not be open to consider someone from out of town if they can find local candidates, consider networking to find a local contact, and with permission, show that person's address in your letter—i.e., your name "care of" your local contact. Once employer contact and interest occurs, try to arrange several interviews on one trip to that town.

If you expect an employer to pick up relocation and travel expenses, you need not mention this in your letter until you are certain about the employer's interest: when you are invited for the interview.

If you are determined to find a job in a specific location and are willing to foot the bill for the move, plan a job search trip to the city in advance, and use this upcoming trip as a way to close the letter:

> I will be in Phoenix from February 14 through 19 and would like to schedule a meeting for that period if possible. I will call to coordinate our schedules.

9. You have a physical impairment.

You fear that a physical disadvantage might stand in the way of a job offer. Don't discuss your handicap in the cover letter. Once an interview is set up, address this issue in a pre-interview power letter.

The major function of a cover letter is to help you get the job interview. If you believe that your impairment will help you get the interview, then by all means mention it in your cover letter. Otherwise, wait.

> I look forward to our interview and the opportunity to discuss my ability to do the work. I will show you how being confined to a wheelchair—which many might consider a handicap—has been no bar to my competency in the field.

10. YOUR SITUATION REQUIRES CONFIDENTIALITY.

Your job searches may be initiated when you are still employed. Although it is customary for the reader of employment inquiries to assume confidentiality, it is a good idea to remind the reader with a sentence such as:

> "Please do not contact my current employer until we have discussed the matter. Thank you."

In answering "blind" or box number advertisements, be very careful about answering directly if your current employer does not know you are in the job market. More than one job seeker has unintentionally sent his resume to his own employer.

11. YOU ARE MAKING THE TRANSITION FROM MILITARY TO CIVILIAN SERVICE.

Indicate the potential for a smooth and marketable transition from military service to the civilian workforce with a paragraph such as this:

> As you will see from my resume, I have served ten years with distinction in the U.S. Navy. This experience has taught me to be very adaptable to rapidly changing situations like yours. My management capabilities will serve your company quite well, and you will also gain the commitment, leadership and responsibility that are inherent in good military personnel. I will be happy to discuss concrete examples of how my naval experience can help you meet your goals.

FIVE

MORE POWER LETTERS

There are many occasions in your job search, and in business in general, when other kinds of power letters besides cover letters are needed. A variety of other types of power letters are discussed below. There are additional sample letters illustrated in Chapter 11.

TO GET INFORMATION

Information is power. The best job searches call for the best and most relevant information. You will collect it from library research, from organizations, and from people in the field. The purpose of this power letter is to get people to respond to your requests for specific information.

WHAT YOU NEED TO KNOW

- **Companies directly involved in the field**
- **Trade and professional associations in the field**
- **Schools specializing in a particular discipline**
- **Relevant articles and books**
- **Names of the people who make hiring decisions**
- **Names of authorities in your chosen field**
- **News about specific companies**
- **New product developments**
- **Mergers and acquisitions**

POINTERS

- Get the name of the person you are making the request of, not just the organization or department.
- Ask first by phone, then confirm your request by mail.
- Acknowledge the institution or person ("I understand your association is one of the most important of its kind..."). If you have read an article by the individual, mention it insightfully in your letter.
- Let the person know how what you are requesting will be useful. ("You can help me get some important leads in the field....")
- If you have specific questions to ask, lay them out one at a time, leaving five to six lines after each so that the respondent can easily write in the answers and return your request to you.
- An alternative approach is to pose the questions in your letter and set a time when you will call to discuss the answers.
- Don't ask for too much. *Wrong:* "Could you please let me know who the top people are in the field of environmental reporting." *Right:* "I am attempting to compile a list of the top four or five people in the field of environmental reporting. Could you please give me some suggestions about how I might identify them. I will call..."

NETWORKING LETTER
(SEE SAMPLE, CHAPTER 11, PAGE 74)

Networking letters are designed to motivate people to help you make the contacts you need to set up meetings and information interviews with job prospects. Most networking letters are to people you know personally or have been introduced to or referred to by someone who knows them. (This might be another employer or a former co-worker, client, or acquaintance.)

In the networking power letter, remind the respondent who you are (if you only met briefly or were referred by a third party) or link yourself with someone the addressee knows and respects. Opening: "We met last year at the Software Publishers conference in Dallas." Or: "Jane Brody praised your achievements in the field and suggested I get in touch with you." You can expand your contacts by asking those in your personal network if they know others who could help you and how to reach them. When a person has gone out of her way to help you, send a thank-you note.

REFERENCE LETTER
(SEE SAMPLE, CHAPTER 11, PAGE 73)

Be prepared to provide references at or after the interview. When asking people to write you a reference letter, be certain they are going to give you a positive reference—some people have been surprised by unexpectedly lukewarm references. Suggest specifically what you'd like your referrers to stress in their letters. If you know the person well enough, you could even draft your own power reference letter for them to use or revise.

FOLLOW-UP LETTER
(SEE SAMPLE, CHAPTER 11, PAGE 78)

Follow up on your cover letters and resumes with phone calls. If the employer ignores your phone call, don't despair. Move forward with something like this: "I respect how busy you are and want to be sure you remember who I am and what I was calling about. Here's a brief recap in writing." At this point, you may repeat some of the things you said in your original cover letter. An alternative approach is simply to send a copy of your original power letter and resume, repeat your desire to have a meeting, and specify the time and date you will call to follow up.

PRE-INTERVIEW LETTER
(SEE SAMPLE, CHAPTER 11, PAGE 79)

By sending a letter timed to arrive a few days before a scheduled interview, you further the momentum of your original power cover letter and resume.

Use a pre-interview letter to set the stage in a way that helps focus the upcoming interview on your strongest capabilities. Show that you have thought about the opportunity and are the kind of person who prepares. Keep it light—not overly directive—and short. A paragraph like this could help set the stage:

> I am looking forward to our meeting next Thursday at two-thirty. I have been thinking about our last conversation and have developed a couple of ideas about the lending opportunity we discussed. I am also anticipating your questions about how I can transfer my public sector experience to the private sector.
>
> I will see you next week...

POST-INTERVIEW LETTER
(SEE SAMPLE, CHAPTER 11, PAGE 80)

After each interview you will want to go beyond the simple "thank you for your time" letter, and compose a power letter designed to further the action and move the hiring process along. Make a clear proposition and a compelling case that supports it. If the next step is a second interview, go for it.

While the interview is fresh in your mind, ask yourself:

- **What kind of person is the company really looking for?**
- **What qualities do I need to strengthen?**
- **What questions could I have asked that I didn't during the interview?**

In your post-interview letter, you can recap the interviewer's comments and reinforce those things that support your compelling case. If issues were raised in the interview that need further clarification or action, go after these. For example:

AGE PROBLEM

If you are an older worker and have reason to believe the interviewer viewed your age negatively, you could say something like:

> My experience in this field has been broad and deep. I have learned much that can be applied to your goals as you described them to me. I am up-to-date with current technology and long-range research. I offer you a depth of experience that only years can bring and a level of commitment supported by imagination and forward thinking.

OTHER CANDIDATES

> I know that you are considering several candidates for this job. I believe I am competitive with the best in the field and look forward to a second meeting after you have had the chance to see the others.

Thank you for being frank with me about your need to postpone the hiring until you are assured of getting the funds for the project. I can understand how crucial this is.

Since I can't guarantee my availability until the final project decision is made, perhaps an alternative can be worked out. I could work with you on a consulting basis for the next three or four months. This would allow you to start your preliminary planning and possibly accumulate more data to support the funding request. It would also allow us to get further acquainted and be ready to launch the project, or if it were called for, formalize our relationship.

I will call you to set up a meeting to discuss this.

STALL LETTER
(SEE SAMPLE, CHAPTER 11, PAGE 83)

A "stall" is the strategy to use when a company has made you an offer, but you want to hear from one or two other potential employers before making your decision.

I very much appreciate the offer and I feel I could contribute significantly to your firm. I will be very involved in another project over the next ten days and would like to schedule a discussion with you then to negotiate the final decision.

After you've sent a delaying letter, you should follow up with a phone call to make sure the employer understands its meaning: you are definitely interested in a final discussion, but you can't do it right now.

RESPONSE TO REJECTION

A rejection is not necessarily the final word. You could see it as part of a process that might lead to later employment with the company or a referral to another job in the company or outside. Use the connections you've made within the company to add to your network and to probe for possible leads elsewhere. A response to a rejection could read something like this:

> I understand you are not now making me an offer. I hope you have found a candidate who is perfect for the assignment.
>
> My own quest for the right position continues, and I would appreciate any feedback or referrals you might have in either another division or in another firm. I hope you won't mind my calling you shortly to get your ideas.

NEGOTIATING TERMS OF ACCEPTANCE
(SEE SAMPLE, CHAPTER 11, PAGE 85)

Don't accept an offer at the time that it's given. Your ability to negotiate on your own behalf demonstrates your finesse and determination.

Be prepared for the negotiation.

- **Know what you can deliver in tangible terms.**
- **Investigate current salary ranges in your field.**
- **Know the competition. Talk to other companies to determine what the current salary ranges are.**
- **Know your strengths and what you can do better than others.**

It is best to conduct your negotiations face-to-face. You can learn a lot from the employer's nonverbal expressions and reactions, knowing when to push harder or when to take a more conservative approach.

If you cannot meet in person, your power letter should focus on reinforcing the value you can contribute to the firm, affirming your interest in the job while keeping the door open to further negotiation.

Thank you for honoring me with your offer. I have been examining several opportunities, however, and feel that we need to discuss the salary and responsibilities of the job further. I very much want to see our relationship work out and look forward to talking with you soon. I will call you....

REJECTING A JOB OFFER WHILE KEEPING THE DOOR OPEN FOR THE FUTURE
(SEE SAMPLE, CHAPTER 11, PAGE 86)

Thank you for offering me the opportunity to contribute to your firm. I know this relationship could be quite successful; however, right now I am more interested in _____. On the other hand, situations change, and I would not be at all surprised if a time might come when I could make a valuable contribution to [name of firm].

SIX
STRATEGIC
CONCERNS

Once you have completed your power letter and resume, it's time to get them into the hands of the decision makers. You will learn about job openings through various avenues and then determine how to proceed.

ADVANCE NOTICE

If you hear about a position before it is announced publicly, respond quickly. First verify the position, and then hand-deliver a cover power letter and resume. Fax your materials only if the utmost urgency is demanded, as you may be sacrificing the quality of their appearance. If you do fax your cover power letter and resume, call the employer's office first to alert them.

TIMING HELP WANTED RESPONSES

When a position is first advertised, the majority of responses arrive two to three days after the ad has run. Then the volume slows down. Employers usually take two to three days to read and digest this material. Time your letter and resume package to arrive four or five business days after the ad has appeared, to improve the chance that it will be read under less hectic conditions. Either mail it or, if you live in the same city, hand-deliver it.

SENDING FOLLOW-UP LETTERS

After each interview, send a follow-up letter so that it arrives in the interviewer's hands within three days. Within that interval, the interviewer, who has probably spoken with other applicants, can still connect you to the job.

The purpose of the follow-up power letter, as discussed earlier, is to reinforce positively what took place at the interview and to increase your chance of being employed or getting the terms or conditions you want from the employer.

RESPONDING TO A BLIND AD

Many people are stymied when they have to respond to a "blind" ad with only a post office box. One concern is that the unnamed employer could be the job seeker's current employer. Another problem is that not knowing who the employer is makes it difficult to customize your approach.

In general, we're not in favor of blind ads. If employers want candidates, they should be willing to say who they are. One strategy around them is to have a neighbor or friend write a fictitious letter in response to the ad, portraying himself as the ideal candidate—a message guaranteed to get a response. Then when the response comes—perhaps a request for an application, you'll learn the name of the company and perhaps even the contact person. You can then research the company before launching your own campaign—and one that will be more competitive.

SEEKING UNADVERTISED OPPORTUNITIES
(SEE SAMPLES, CHAPTER II, PAGES 72, 74, 84)

At any given time the majority of opportunities are not advertised. This is the "hidden" job market. The recommended approach is to select a dozen or so companies that usually employ people in the position you seek, find out something about each organization, and send a custom-tailored letter and resume to each. It's better to send fewer well-researched power letters when seeking a hidden job than to "blitz" the field with hundreds of weak letters.

USING A LETTER AS YOUR RESUME

There are certain instances when you might not want to send your resume to an employer: when your resume shows a spotty work history or your background is in a totally different field.

In these situations, a good letter can serve as your resume. Expand the information about your background, skills, and experience and relate them very closely to the job you are seeking and the needs of the employer. This approach allows you to focus directly on the employer's needs.

> Dear Ms. Trent,
>
> I was intrigued by the recent news articles published about your new software programs to aid in teaching English as a second language. This innovation will go far in allowing people to learn at their own speed in the right educational settings. In my work in ESL in New York schools, we often wished for such learning tools.
>
> Given my five years of work in a related project, I believe that I could help you get funding for a major pilot program to help launch this idea.
>
> I will call you in the next few days to see if we can arrange a meeting to discuss these opportunities further.

The power letter-resume alternative is useful if you are returning to the workforce after a long absence. For example, a woman returning to the workforce after having spent several years raising a child should include a paragraph like this in her power letter:

> I'm writing a letter rather than sending you a detailed resume because I have spent the last seven years raising a child and, generally, being a homemaker. A traditional resume form would not reflect my capabilities as much as I hope this letter will.

COMBINING PHONE AND LETTER

A phone call can be as powerful or more powerful than a letter. But one disadvantage of the phone is that the employer can forget what's been said, whereas your written communication is preserved.

In many cases you should use the phone call and the power letter together. For example, before you send a follow-up letter after a job interview, call the interviewer and say something like: "I enjoyed our meeting and I'm putting together some questions and reactions to the interview. I'll send these over to you in a day or two."

Another time to precede a letter with a phone call is when you've heard about a position by word of mouth. In this situation, you could call the employer and say something like this: "I've heard about your opening for a _____ and would like to send you some information. I have one or two questions to ask first." Use this to gain information that will help you focus your letter and resume.

Another way to use the phone to your advantage is to get to know the secretary of the employer and remember her or his name. Once you establish contact, it will be easier to call back and say something like: "Hi, it's [your name]. I'd like to get some information to [the interviewer], and wonder if I send it to you, can you make sure she gets it?"

RESPONDING TO REQUESTS FOR SALARY HISTORY

Many employment advertisements request information about your past salary. This can present you with a dilemma: how to be competitively "priced" and still leave room for negotiation.
To decide how to address this issue, consider:

1. Are you comfortable with the possibility that several real opportunities will be available to you?

2. Do you need to make a special attempt to discuss your salary before revealing it?

If you answer yes to the first question and are confident in going for a higher compensation package right from the start, be upfront about your demands: "My most recent compensation was over _____, and I look forward to an opportunity that gives me increased responsibility."

If you don't feel your most recent salary reflects your true worth, don't include salary information in the letter and say something like: "My salary requirements are competitive with the current market." Or:

> I acknowledge your request for salary requirements and feel that it would be more appropriate to discuss this in person as I learn more about the requirements of the job.

If you are in a field where the salary range is narrow, for example, executive secretary, administrative assistant, or clerk-typist, then request something toward the top third of the accepted range in your power letter.

DRAWING THE LINE BETWEEN ASSERTIVE AND BOASTFUL

When you speak positively about yourself in your power letter, make sure you connect your assertion to what you believe you can contribute to the employer's goals. Don't emphasize what you can do that another cannot. Convey your strengths without belittling others.

FAX

You should not fax a cover letter or resume to a potential employer unless time is crucial or it is requested. After you have established a relationship, it may be appropriate to fax certain types of letters, such as a list of questions you would like answered, or a pre-interview power letter. If you send a letter or document by fax, send a good original by mail and indicate this on the fax. Avoid sending multi-page documents by fax unless they are requested.

OVERNIGHT MAIL

If the situation is not urgent, using overnight mail services might be interpreted as a sign of extravagance—or even mild panic on your part. On the other hand, if you are trying to reach an individual who you know will be out of town, or you know that a decision is pending, it's a good idea to use expedited mail to deliver your material.

SEVEN

COMMUNICATING YOUR BEST

Capability is the "currency" of careers. Tomorrow's jobs go to the most qualified—those who have the skills and qualities that meet the employer's needs.

The key to career success is the creation of value in the eyes of the employer. The more the employer believes he or she will benefit from hiring you, the more opportunities for better jobs and salaries will open to you.

By working through the exercises in this chapter and Chapter 8, you will develop a vocabulary to describe your capabilities and accomplishments that will empower your letters. Here is a list of the exercises included in the next two chapters.

CHAPTER 7

1. Capability Detector—pages 45–46. Prepare an inventory of your strongest capabilities.
2. Capability Statements—page 47. Craft statements that describe your best.
3. Leadership Qualities—pages 48–49. Add qualities of leadership.
4. Your Accomplishments—pages 50–52. Pick the best accomplishments to include in your letters.

CHAPTER 8

YOUR UNIQUE SELLING POINTS—WORKSHEET

1. What job are you going for
2. Target company/division
3. Imagine yourself as an employer
4. Personal qualities
5. Selling points
6. Compelling examples

CAPABILITY DETECTOR

Identify the capabilities you have that an employer would look for in a successful candidate. Review the list of verbs below and check any word that relates to something you believe you can contribute. Check as many as apply; you can pare them down later.

I CAN...

accelerate	contribute	distribute
achieve	control	draw
acquire	coordinate	draw up
administer	correspond	edit
analyze	counsel	eliminate
arbitrate	create	establish
advise	criticize	evaluate
assist	delegate	examine
arrange	deliver	execute
assemble	demonstrate	expand
audit	design	expedite
broaden	detect	formulate
budget	determine	generate
build	develop	guide
calculate	devise	hire
chart	diagnose	identify
collect	direct	implement
complete	discover	improve
compose	dispense	increase
conceive	disprove	initiate

___ install   ___ plan   ___ review

___ institute   ___ prepare   ___ revise

___ instruct   ___ prescribe   ___ reward

___ interpret   ___ present   ___ route

___ interview   ___ prevent   ___ save

___ invent   ___ process   ___ select

___ investigate   ___ produce   ___ sell

___ launch   ___ program   ___ serve

___ lead   ___ promote   ___ set up

___ lecture   ___ propose   ___ sing

___ log   ___ protect   ___ solve

___ maintain   ___ provide   ___ strategize

___ manage   ___ purchase   ___ structure

___ monitor   ___ receive   ___ study

___ motivate   ___ recommend   ___ supervise

___ navigate   ___ record   ___ supply

___ negotiate   ___ recruit   ___ teach

___ network   ___ reduce   ___ test

___ observe   ___ refer   ___ train

___ obtain   ___ render   ___ translate

___ operate   ___ report   ___ upgrade

___ order   ___ represent   ___ utilize

___ organize   ___ research   ___ win

___ oversee   ___ restore   ___ work with

___ perform   ___ reverse   ___ write

CAPABILITY STATEMENTS

Now select from the verb roots defined above those that might be most useful to the letters you will write, and as an exercise, write four or five complete statements that could be used to define your value to a potential employer.

In regard to the job as

_____

I can...

_____

_____

_____

_____

In regard to the job as

_____

I can...

_____

_____

_____

In regard to the job as

_____

I can...

_____

_____

_____

_____

Use this approach and the following to help you find the best vocabulary to describe your value to future employers.

LEADERSHIP QUALITIES

Companies today are facing dramatic change and need leadership qualities as well as skills and capabilities. Leadership qualities distinguish you from run-of-the-mill candidates. Here is a list of leadership qualities that reflect what many companies involved in change and transition look for in new job applicants.

Check any term you think would strengthen your appeal as a leader and could be woven into your letters.

___360-degree thinker
___accepting
___achievement-oriented
___adaptive
___always learning
___ambitious
___analytical
___assertive
___attentive -
___authentic
___candid
___capable
___caring
___challenging
___coaching
___collaborative -
___committed
___commonsensical
___communications-oriented
___community-minded
___competitive
___conflict-resolving
___consensus-building
___consistent
___continuously improving
___cost conscious
___courageous
___creative

___customer-focused ~
___dedicated
___detail-oriented
___determined
___diligent ~
___diplomatic
___direct
___discreet
___economical
___efficient
___empowering
___energetic
___energizing
___enterprising
___entrepreneurial
___expressive
___fence-building
___flexible
___focused ~
___generous
___good under stress
___hardworking
___helpful
___high energy
___high-performing
___honest
___idealistic
___imaginative

___individualistic
___influential
___informed
___innovative
___insightful
___intuitive
___inventive
___magnetic
___mobile
___motivating
___numbers savvy
___objective
___observant
___open
___optimistic
___out front
___outgoing
___patient
___perceptive
___persistent
___persuasive
___polished
___positive
___practical
___precise
___principled
___productive
___professional
___public-spirited

___quality conscious
___reliable
___resolving
___resourceful
___responsible
___results-oriented
___sales-oriented
___self-confident
___self-directed
___self-disciplined
___sensitive
___service-oriented
___sociable
___spirited
___strategic
___strong
___supportive
___task-oriented
___team-building
___team player
___technological
___thorough
___trustworthy
___unafraid
___values-driven
___versatile
___visionary
___willing to learn
___willing to change

Add your own:

_____

_____

_____

_____

Your Accomplishments

Accomplishments are results, contributions, or achievements you have produced. You have produced accomplishments in every area of you life: past or current jobs, school projects, volunteer work. They create a positive picture and are hard to ignore.

To start thinking about your accomplishments, check any word that reminds you of something valuable you have done.

I HAVE...

___ accelerated	___ contributed	___ eliminated
___ achieved	___ controlled	___ established
___ acquired	___ coordinated	___ evaluated
___ administered	___ corresponded	___ examined
___ advised	___ counseled	___ executed
___ analyzed	___ created	___ expanded
___ arbitrated	___ criticized	___ expedited
___ arranged	___ delegated	___ formulated
___ assembled	___ delivered	___ generated
___ assisted	___ demonstrated	___ guided
___ audited	___ designed	___ hired
___ broadened	___ detected	___ identified
___ budgeted	___ determined	___ implemented
___ built	___ developed	___ improved
___ calculated	___ devised	___ increased
___ charted	___ diagnosed	___ initiated
___ collected	___ directed	___ installed
___ completed	___ discovered	___ instituted
___ composed	___ dispensed	___ instructed
___ conceived	___ disproved	___ introduced
___ conducted	___ distributed	___ interpreted
___ conserved	___ drawn	___ interviewed
___ constructed	___ drawn up	___ invented
___ consulted	___ edited	___ investigated

___ launched	___ prevented	___ revised
___ led	___ processed	___ rewarded
___ lectured	___ produced	___ routed
___ logged	___ programmed	___ saved
___ maintained	___ promoted	___ selected
___ managed	___ proposed	___ sold
___ monitored	___ protected	___ served
___ motivated	___ provided	___ set up
___ navigated	___ purchased	___ solved
___ negotiated	___ received	___ strategized
___ networked	___ recommended	___ structured
___ observed	___ recorded	___ studied
___ obtained	___ recruited	___ supervised
___ operated	___ reduced	___ supplied
___ ordered	___ referred	___ taught
___ organized	___ rendered	___ tested
___ overseen	___ reported	___ trained
___ performed	___ represented	___ translated
___ planned	___ researched	___ upgraded
___ prepared	___ restored	___ utilized
___ prescribed	___ reversed	___ won
___ presented	___ reviewed	___ worked

Now, using some of the words you selected, list the five or more specific accomplishments that in a cover letter or resume you might want to bring to the attention of a prospective employer.

Employer Prospect: _____

Key accomplishments to highlight:

_____

_____

_____

Employer Prospect: _____

Key accomplishments to highlight:

_____

_____

_____

Employer Prospect: _____

Key accomplishments to highlight:

_____

_____

_____

Employer Prospect: _____

Key accomplishments to highlight:

_____

_____

_____

EIGHT

YOUR
UNIQUE
SELLING
POINTS

WORKSHEET

The following information should be gathered for each new job opportunity you pursue. It can be included in a variety of power letters—cover letter, pre-interview letter, follow-up letter and more. You may make copies of this form for future power letters.

1. WHAT JOB ARE YOU GOING FOR?

_____

2. TARGET COMPANY/DIVISION

Name_____

- What does it do?

- What are the company's objectives?

- What has the company accomplished recently?

- What is its competition?

- What factors influence the company's success?

- What are the company's most pressing problems and challenges?

3. IMAGINE YOURSELF AS AN EMPLOYER.

You must hire someone right away as a
_____ (enter your specific job target).

You want the best person in this job—someone who will help you make your business or department a success. It must be someone who will help you with many day-to-day problems and tasks. Five of the most important *challenges* are:

(a) _____

(b) _____

(c) _____

(d) _____

(e) _____ .

To solve these day-to-day challenges, you need someone with the right knowledge, training, skills and abilities. The best candidate would have these *capabilities*:

(f) _____

(g) _____

(h) _____

(i) _____

(j) _____ .

4. PERSONAL QUALITIES

It takes a person with the right character and personality to perform well on this job. These include the *qualities*:

(k) _____

(l) _____

(m) _____

(n) _____

(o) _____ .

5. SELLING POINTS

Review your answers and select the most important personal selling points to include in your power letters.
Consider the following:

What are the specific ways you can contribute to the company's success?

_____

_____

How can you offer far more value than the job description requires?

_____

_____

What innovations in technology can you bring to the job?

_____

_____

What can you do to accomplish the job more efficiently or at a lower cost?

_____

_____

How could you more actively serve the company's customers?

_____

_____

What can you do to motivate others to attain a higher level of performance and satisfaction?

_____

_____

_____

You Are Valuable to an Employer Because You Can...

Generate revenues
Cut costs
Increase productivity
Be innovative
Improve quality

Save time
Focus on customers
Use technology
Motivate others
Transform problems
  into opportunities

COMPELLING EXAMPLES OF YOUR UNIQUE SELLING POINTS

Support your unique selling points with a compelling case—examples of successes that relate to this employer. Some examples: use any you want for future power letters:

*You have worked on problems similar to those the employer faces, and from different perspectives.

*You have knowledge of a particular technology that can ease bottlenecks, reduce costs, and speed service.

*Your particular combination of training and experience makes you especially qualified to serve the employer's vision.

*You understand the competitive situation in detail.

*You have talked to customers and know their concerns.

*You comprehend the underlying issues in the industry or company.

*Your qualitative self-assessment projects you far ahead of those with otherwise similar qualities (integrity, persistence, leadership, etc.).

*You understand a particular market thoroughly and could give the employer access to it.

*You rise to a challenge and will not give up until it's met.

Your own list of compelling examples :

SUMMARY STATEMENTS

Review the key capabilities, competencies and accomplishments you identified in Chapter 7 and the company's needs and your unique selling points from this chapter, and complete statements to use in future letters that clearly communicate your skills, knowledge and ability to do the job.

Regarding my job target as a _____

_____

I can:_____

_____

because I have:_____

_____

Regarding my job target as a _____

_____

I can:_____

_____

because I have:_____

_____

Regarding my job target as a _____

_____

I can:_____

_____

because I have:_____

_____

Regarding my job target as a _____

_____

I can:_____

_____

because I have:_____

_____

NINE

POWER
PARAGRAPHS

On the following pages we have provided a variety of sample paragraphs for power letters. Peruse them for ideas when you are writing your own letters.

POWER OPENINGS

COVER LETTER

I saw your notice in the _____, and I would like to apply for the _____ position. As you will see from my resume, the qualities you need closely match the ones I've developed in my career.

The article in _____ about your company's _____ was very impressive. Congratulations. I'm pleased to see a firm get public recognition for its commitment to _____. In my enclosed resume you will see how....

_____ suggested that since my background is in _____, I get in touch with you to find out how I can best contribute to your company's work in _____.

Since I work in the _____ field, I'm well aware of your company's strong reputation in _____ and _____.

I'm writing to colleagues such as you to ask if you know of any career opportunities in the _____ field where a person with my _____ and _____ skills could make a contribution.

As a leader in the field, I admire your work in _____. I have been following your progress in _____, for _____ years.

I am moving to _____, and I understand that your company is one of the area's leading firms in _____ and _____.

According to _____ (*contact person/cite reading material*), I understand that you are considering _____ (*goals, projects, direction*), and may be in the market for someone who can provide strong leadership in pursuit of this goal.

POWER OPENINGS FOR FOLLOW-UP LETTERS

It was a pleasure to meet with you on _____ about your opening for a _____.

Thank you for taking the time to meet with me on _____ about the _____ position. During the interview, I learned that the qualities you need are a close match to the ones I've developed in my career.

Our personal meeting on _____ regarding the _____ position enlightened me further on the qualities you are looking for.

As a result of our meeting about the _____ position on _____, I now have greater insight into the needs of your firm, and of my ability to meet those needs. I would now like to take a few more minutes of your valuable time to present this information.

Thank you for taking the time to meet with me about the _____ position at your firm. While I realize that the position is highly competitive, I would like to take just a moment more to review my unique skills with you and how they could directly benefit your firm.

I am writing to follow up on the initial inquiry I sent to you on _____. At the time, I forwarded a cover letter and resume to you that highlighted my _____ and _____ in response to your _____ opening. I appreciate the time you spent on _____ discussing the _____ position with me. At the time, you had mentioned contacting me on _____. Because I understand how demanding your job must be, and I had not heard from you, I would like to take this opportunity to once again let you know what I can offer you in return for a position in your department.

I would like to thank you for the opportunity to meet you in person to discuss the _____ position. Since I have not yet heard from you since we met on _____, I wanted to let you know that I am still a willing candidate for the position. I would like to recap briefly the unique skills I can offer your firm.

POWER PROPOSITIONS
COVER LETTER

I believe that with your reputation as a _____, and my fresh insight into _____, I would be of value to you right away in _____ .

Since I'm entering the field of_____ with a background in _____, and particular experience in _____, I believe my unique skills would support the company's continued growth and success.

Because I have _____ years of direct experience in _____, I believe you could utilize my _____ skills in meeting the needs of your company.

I have just graduated from _____ with a degree in _____, and given your work in _____, I would like to offer my talent as a _____ to benefit your firm's _____ goals.

Since my background is in _____, _____ believes that I could make a significant contribution to _____.

_____ feels that my skills and experience in _____ could be of use to you right away.

If you need someone who can _____, I believe I would make a significant difference at _____.

While my hourly commitment would not be full-time, the experience and skills in _____ and _____ that I can bring to the position will reflect _____ years in the field of _____.

POWER PROPOSITIONS FOR FOLLOW-UP LETTERS

As we discussed during the interview, I believe my unique skills as a ＿＿＿＿ and a ＿＿＿＿ would promote the company's continued growth and success with your new ＿＿＿＿ product.

I am more convinced now than ever that my contributions as a ＿＿＿＿ would add to the future success of your company.

Again, I'd like to propose that with your reputation as a ＿＿＿＿, and my fresh insight into ＿＿＿＿, I could be of value to you right away on the ＿＿＿＿ account.

Since our discussion, I have felt confident that with my ＿＿＿＿ years of experience in ＿＿＿＿, you could be able to put my ＿＿＿＿ skills to work in your ＿＿＿＿ department.

POWER CASES

These are simply general examples. In order to make your own letters most compelling, you will need to use the data you collected on your unique selling points.

COVER LETTER—COMPLETE SAMPLE

During the three years that I've worked at the Bread Basket, the bakery has quadrupled in size. During that period, as head baker and production manager, I was responsible for numerous changes in production, including training employees on the spiral mixer, retarder and proof box, and the Winkler oven.

Working with a small group of employees, I have managed to fill the growing demand for our bread without sacrificing quality. In fact, despite the increase in demand, I was able to stay in touch with our wide variety of customers and create six new breads based on their needs. As a result, we've increased bread sales 6 to 8 percent. We currently operate seven days a week, sixteen to eighteen hours a day, and produce 5,000 to 8,000 loaves of bread per day.

In _____, I will be receiving a _____ degree in _____ from _____. Throughout my academic career, I have had a special interest in the area of _____. My studies of _____ have been especially rewarding and now I would like to offer my abilities as a professional in the field. *(Add your unique selling points.)*

For the past _____ years, I have worked as a _____ with _____. During this time, I have acquired experience in _____ and earned recognition for _____. I am especially proud of _____. *(Add your unique selling points.)*

My _____ years of academic experience should demonstrate my reliability and goal orientation. *(Add your unique selling points.)*

My involvement in _____ has provided opportunities to practice the skills of _____ and _____. I understand that these capabilities are important to a firm that excels in _____. *(Add your unique selling points.)*

Throughout my career as a _____ , I have had the opportunity to hone my problem-solving skills. In particular, I've learned how to facilitate _____ and _____. These abilities prove vital when I _____. *(Add your unique selling points.)*

As a _____, I feel I have two unique benefits to offer: _____ and _____. Throughout my career, these qualities have produced an increase in _____. They have also encouraged others to _____. *(Add your unique selling points.)*

I know that a _____ has to have the quality of _____ , and I know that quality is important to your firm. It's a characteristic that I've worked on throughout my career. My _____ and _____ have produced consistent _____.
(Add your unique selling points.)

My _____ years of work in _____ should be unique among your applicants. I feel my combination of _____ skills and on-the-job experience are an ideal match for your needs. *(Add your unique selling points.)*

Throughout my career, I have worked on my ability to _____. The results in _____ have won acclaim from _____ and _____. In particular, I am proud of the _____ where I _____. *(Add your unique selling points.)*

When I was _____, I developed a successful _____. This important project brought my employer a _____ percent increase in sales. After studying your firm, I feel that I could achieve similar results after a period of _____. *(Add your unique selling points.)*

In my experience with _____, I've had to learn new _____ and _____ quickly but thoroughly. If training in _____ and _____ is necessary then for success with your firm, I'm ready. *(Add your unique selling points.)*

Although it has been several years since I worked with _____, I believe that my ability to _____ and _____ will prove valuable. The new opening sounds like a perfect opportunity to offer these skills as a _____ in the company. *(Add your unique selling points.)*

COMPELLING CASES—INTERVIEW FOLLOW-UP LETTERS

Once again, I'd like to highlight the unique benefits I have to offer as a _____. During my _____ years in the field, I was able to _____ and _____. I think the experiences I gained will be of immeasurable value to your firm should you decide to hire me as a _____. *(Add your unique selling points.)*

While we did not get much time during the interview to touch upon the _____ skills I acquired as a _____, in retrospect, I now think that these are the kind of skills that are required for the job you described. When I was a _____, I was able to develop _____ and _____ to the satisfaction of my former employers. In particular, I am proud of having been able to _____ for _____.

During our interview, we discussed the company's need for _____ and _____. I'd like to take another moment to review the unique contributions I've made to my past employers. *(Add your unique selling points.)* Given the opportunity to succeed in your company, I believe I can offer the same results.

Having met with you in person, I now understand what skills your company seeks in an employee. As you review my job history, you will see that I have developed the same skills you seek. As a _____, I have demonstrated _____ and _____ qualities over a period of _____ years. I have assisted past employers with _____ and _____, and am most proud of _____. *(Add your unique selling points.)*

POWER CLOSINGS

COVER LETTER

I am confident that my knowledge and abilities would be of value to your company. I would like to request a few minutes of your time to discuss my qualifications. I will contact you on _____ to arrange a meeting. If you have any questions in the meantime, please call me at _____.

Although I know your time is valuable, I would appreciate a few minutes to discuss my qualifications and how they can directly benefit your company. I will contact you on _____ to set up a meeting. Please call me at _____ if you have any questions.

I would appreciate a chance to meet with you and discuss how my skills could assist your firm in its goal to _____. I will be in the area on _____ and will call you on _____ to see if there is a convenient time we can meet during my stay. If this time won't work for you, please call me at _____.

Your commitment to _____ and my willingness to _____ look like a strong match. I'm sure this relationship will be good for the growth of the company. I will contact you on _____ to arrange a meeting to discuss the possibilities. Please don't hesitate to contact me should you wish to reach me before this date.

POWER CLOSINGS FOR FOLLOW-UP LETTERS

Once again I'd like to thank you for meeting with me to discuss the _____ position. Because I believe you will consider me an active candidate, I will call back on _____ to check on the status of my application. In the meantime, please feel free to call me at _____ if you have any questions.

I sincerely appreciate the time you took to meet with me about the current opening in your department. I would like to reiterate my continued commitment to offering your company my unique skills. I will check with your office in the next week to find out whether or not I'm still in the race. In the meantime, please feel free to call me should you seek references and/or recommendations.

TEN
FINDING FACTS FAST

Is a company you want to work for currently expanding its work-force, contracting it, or staying the same?

What is the stock of the company selling for today compared with a year ago? Has its value gone up or down?

Does the company intend to open new branches in foreign cities?

What is the name of the top executive in the department of the company you would want to work for, and how can you reach that person by phone?

Does the company have plans soon to merge with another firm?

Being able to answer these questions—and many others—about a target company helps you decide whether it makes sense to approach that company and how to write a power opening that will insure that your letter is read, and eventually, that you get that job interview.

Today you can use computer technology to quickly find facts about almost any organization—public or private. And of course, if you cannot find what you need to know using computers, you can fall back on traditional sources, such as print publications and the telephone.

The purpose of this chapter is to give you a brief guided tour of some of the major computer-based and other resources you can use to find facts fast about almost any company.

COMPUTER TECHNOLOGIES
AND SERVICES

CD-ROM Products

A CD-ROM is a disk that looks like a music CD, only it can hold 500 megabytes of text or more—a virtual encyclopedia of information that you can instantly boot up on the computer screen, read, print out, or save.

Using a CD-ROM that contains the full text of *New York Times* articles for the past three years, for example, you could instruct the computer to search for "General Motors," and in a few seconds have available every article from the *Times* in that three-year period that discussed GM. You would have a treasury of names of executives and facts about the company that you could use when writing your power letters.

Most libraries today have CD-ROM disks you can borrow free of charge, and dozens of titles are available commercially for use on your own computer. To be a good searcher takes know-how and practice, but almost anyone can begin searching immediately. Librarians can help you refine your search so that you are certain to get "hits," and that your subject is not so broad that you retrieve unwieldy amounts of information or so narrow that you miss valuable material.

In general, CD-ROM provides you with two kinds of information. The first is full text, which means that you retrieve and print out articles just as they appeared in a newspaper or magazine. The other is simply bibliographic. At a minimum, it tells you the name of the article, author(s), publication, and year and date of publication. You can then go directly to the periodical or other printed document to read the contents.

Sometimes, just the title of an article can tell you what you need to know. For example, if a headline reads, "General Motors Cutting Its Workforce Across the Board by 20%," you might decide this is not the best time to seek work with GM. In addition to "bare bones" document retrieval information, some bibliographic CD-ROMs are annotated—they give you a brief summary of the text of the article.

Among the many CD-ROM titles you can use free of charge in libraries are the following:

The National Newspaper Index
The New York Times
The Wall Street Journal
InfoTrak
ABI/Inform
Current periodicals
Dun & Bradstreet

Ask your librarian for other titles.

ONLINE SERVICES

Online services are providers and distributors of information that you can access using your computer and a modem. Many services tie into the Internet, currently the chief network on the information highway. Some of the online services you can use to find facts fast about employing organizations are:

CompuServe
America Online
Dialog
Dun & Bradstreet (D&B)
Nexis
Standard and Poor (S&P)
CDB Infotek

A general online service such as CompuServe or America Online is a "gateway" to hundreds of databases, or libraries of information, allowing you access to the text of literally thousands of journals, newspapers, newsletters, and other publications. The information they provide can help you write the best power letters and target appropriate employers. On CompuServe, for example, for background information on companies and recent news, you can search the following:

- **Business Database Plus**—provides full text citations from 500 business magazines, journals and specialized newsletters.
- **Executive News Service Plus**—provides stories filed within the most recent 24 hours by the major wire services, including Associated Press (AP), United Press International (UPI), and Reuters.
- **Newspaper Library**—provides full-text articles from 55 newspapers in the United States.
- **Business Dateline**—provides full-text articles from 115 regional business publications in the United States and Canada.
- **Disclosure II**—provides financial information, ownership detail, and business segment data on publicly traded companies.
- **S&P Online**—provides company research reports, background financial information, and historic and current price information on publicly traded companies.
- **D&B Dun's Market Identifiers**—provides background information, including sales, number of employees, and net worth on more than 7 million businesses located in the United States with more than 98 percent of the records representing privately held companies.
- **TRW Business Profiles**—provides key business facts, company sizes, ownership information and product descriptions for both public and private companies.

To get information from online services, you have to be a subscriber. Subscription rates generally run from around $10.00 to $50.00 per month, and there are often additional charges for accessing certain libraries, downloading files, printing, and connect time. If you are not a subscriber and do not want to be, you can have a friend who subscribes help you get information or hire a professional information provider to get you the facts you need.

The major advantage of using online services over CD-ROM products for finding facts about companies is that the former provides the most up-to-date information. A CD-ROM product, such as *The New York Times* or *Current Periodicals*, for example, issues updates quarterly or semi-annually; but using an online service, you can obtain yesterday's information in many instances, or get information that is only a few days or a week old.

Some public libraries will do an online search for you, but

they will charge in almost every instance. This is a good investment—it will save you the cost of becoming a subscriber, and, of course, of buying a computer and modem if you do not already own this equipment.

NONCOMPUTER RESEARCH

In some instances, you may find that doing your research in the library and on the telephone is the best way to find out what you want to know about a company. A few phone calls can get you the names of people currently holding down jobs in key organizations, whereas almost every other form of research is quickly dated.

If you plan research of print materials and have access to a library, you should know that there are bound indexes to just about every publication that has appeared in print. For example, the *Reader's Guide to Current Periodicals* can help you track down articles in magazines, *The New York Times Index* can lead you to articles that have appeared in the *Times* since it began publication, and Dun & Bradstreet and Standard and Poor directories of companies are available in printed form. With such a wealth of reference material available, your best approach is to visit a good library and ask the librarian to help you focus your search.

The worst drawback to using printed directories, however, is that they are often out of date. Check the date of publication on one of the front pages to make sure you are not using an out-of-date directory.

Other sources that could be of value to you in your job search and power letters are company-produced publications, such as newsletters, intra-organization memorandums, and in-house magazines. Often these don't show up on any CD-ROM product or online service, and yet they can be extremely informative about what is going on within the company at present. Inquire directly at the company or, if you have a contact, ask her to pick up a few of the most recent issues.

ELEVEN

POWER
LETTER
HALL
OF
FAME

On the following pages we have provided you with fifteen examples of good power letters covering a variety of situations. Use these as a practical review of the principles you have learned in this book.

As you continue in your future career, we hope that your use of this material will increase your success. Good luck.

FIFTEEN JOB-WINNING POWER LETTERS

1. Mark Johnson — Telemarketing Manager—out-of-town visit
2. Maria Ricci — Youth Counselor—reference letter
3. William Cooper — Military Transition—networking letter
4. Harvey Regenbogen — Fundraising Associate—cover letter
5. David Gillam — Sales Representative—part-time to full-time
6. Shane Jamar — Computer Operator–Finance—career shift
7. Nils Ebert — Marketing Associate—follow-up
8. Sarina Coleman — Stockbroker—pre-interview
9. Richard Ellsworth — Travel Consultant—return from retirement— follow-up
10. Ellen Springer — Paralegal—homemaker returning—follow-up
11. Beth Ross — Project Manager—position deferred
12. Pete Stokes — Engineer—to stall an answer
13. Rhonda Jackson — Merchandising Manager—pinpointed cover letter
14. Jane Beamer — Art Director—salary negotiation
15. Salvatore Albano — Baker—turndown—keeping door open

MARK JOHNSON
Telemarketing Manager

Mark Johnson was successfully employed as a telemarketing manager until his firm had to cut back drastically and his position was eliminated. Then his wife's job was transferred to a new city and the Johnsons decided to make the move. Because Mark didn't have time to wait for an opportunity to come to him, he collected names of telemarketing companies in the new city, researched those companies, and then sent out a customized letter to each one.

Dear Ms. Reanot:

I am moving to Seattle and I understand that, as director of telemarketing, you are the person to ask about how I might best offer my ten years of telemarketing experience to your department.

Recent articles in <u>Wired</u> have pointed to the vast influence your company has had on the development of sophisticated customer outreach, and I believe that it is in this specific area that I could make a significant contribution to Teleworld Consultants.

As a telemarketing manager, I have honed my ability to produce results in a competitive climate. I was able to create new leads and set appointments for our sales force as well as train and supervise new telemarketers. After studying your firm, I feel I could offer articulate leadership and develop the high-quality fresh leads you've been looking for.

I would appreciate the opportunity to discuss my skills with you in detail and explore how they would be of value to Teleworld. I will be in the area the week of January 10th and will call you to arrange an informational meeting. If this is not convenient, and you'd like to get in touch with me in the meantime, please call.

MARIA RICCI
Youth Counselor

Maria had worked as a youth-group counselor for ten years when she decided she wanted to move on. She sent a cover letter and resume out to a new company and was granted an interview. The interviewer asked her to bring a letter of reference. Maria met with her former boss and told her which qualities and capabilities she wanted to stress. The following letter, though written by her former boss, was the result of Maria's assertive input.

Dear Mr. Feld:

I was Maria Ricci's former supervisor at Joylene, and I am writing to recommend Maria and the skills she can bring to your Youth Action Project.

Because many of the approaches Maria used during her six years with Joylene are similar to yours, I believe her ten years as a youth counselor will be invaluable in helping the area youth in a positive and loving manner.

I have supervised counselors in Marionville for twenty years, and I can honestly say that the programs run by Maria had some of the highest success rates and were among the center's most popular courses, due mostly to the fact that Maria instilled such confidence in all the children. An informal survey conducted last year showed that youths in the Marionville program were far less likely than others to get in trouble or leave school.

I highly recommend Maria for this position. Please feel free to call me with any questions.

WILLIAM COOPER

Military Transition

William wanted to transfer his military experience to the private sector, and because he had a lot of contacts in the business community, he decided that rather than respond to advertisements, he would first put out the word that he was looking for work.

Dear Mr. Brender:

We met last April at a recruiting convention in Seattle, and at the time, we discussed the exciting growth your company had seen in online computer services. I've kept abreast of that development and would like to congratulate you on a job well done in a competitive market.

I am now planning to transfer the skills I developed as an officer at one of the largest communications stations in the U.S. Air Force into the private sector, and I am writing to ask if you know of any career opportunities that would utilize my expertise in organizational development and management, or if you could recommend some people to contact for leads. I have enclosed my recent resume.

During my five years as development officer at the Air Force Station in Tulsa, Oklahoma—where I oversaw a staff of thirty-two and a $1.3 million budget—I managed consulting services and facilities. I developed a successful marketing plan that achieved a 37 percent growth in retention.

I believe that given the opportunity, I could offer the private sector the same winning results. Because I value your ideas, I would welcome a chance to speak with you in person. I will call you next week to set up an appointment, but please feel free to call me in the meantime should you have any questions. Thank you for your time and interest.

HARVEY REGENBOGEN
Fundraising Associate

Harvey Regenbogen had worked for three years as a fundraiser specializing in the performing arts. He felt ready to move up to associate, but there was no opportunity for advancement in his current job. So Harvey responded to an ad in his local paper for a fundraising associate. Before he wrote the letter, he called the organization, and through the secretary, got the name of the person who was going to do the hiring. Harvey also researched the company to find out where he could best offer his skills.

Dear Mr. Federoff:

I spoke to Jean Simon today, who was kind enough to direct me to you regarding the advertised opening for an associate fundraiser. The skills you need closely match the ones I've developed in my career.

I have three years of experience in art fundraising, and I'm sure my skills could be put to good use in your present capital campaign.

When I was a fundraiser for the Children's Museum, I coordinated special events, managed volunteers, and handled donor and prospective donor research. I have a B.A. in art history, strong computer skills and excellent written and verbal skills.

I am confident that after you review my resume, and we have the opportunity to speak, you will be convinced that my knowledge and abilities will be of value to your company. I would appreciate the opportunity to discuss my qualifications with you in person. I will contact you on February 1st to arrange a meeting. If you have any questions, please call me at...

DAVID GILLAM
Sales Representative

When David, a graduating senior, heard through the grapevine that there was an unadvertised sales opening at the company where he'd been an intern for several summers, he sent a cover letter in which he transferred several years of solid internship experiences into a full-time job target.

Dear Ms. Adler:

Now that the word is out about the opening for a Boise sales representative for Clearwater Systems, I'd like to put in my bid for the position.

Having spent three summers in sales positions at Clearwater, and having just graduated from Iowa State University with a B.A. in communication arts, I've developed into a first-rate professional communicator who can help boost your sales.

As an intern for Clearwater, I proved that I can sell and promote on cold calls by establishing a good new customer base in a short period of time. In 1993 I was the proud recipient of the Gold Seal award for the most consistent growth in repeat business. That was a great thrill for me!

I would like to meet you for a discussion of my skills and how I can continue to benefit Clearwater. I will contact you next week to arrange an interview later in the month.

SHANE JAMAR
Computer Operator–Finance

Shane was working as a bookkeeper by day and taking classes in computer applications at night. After two years of study, he felt ready to make a career change. Since no specific computer openings were being advertised, Shane pared down the field to those positions that would require a background in bookkeeping and finance. Then he researched the companies within that narrower scope, got the names of treasurers and chief financial officers, and sent out customized letters.

Dear Mr. Enger:

I have heard about your recent merger with Ingersoll. I imagine that a major effort has now begun to consolidate the financial departments of both firms.

I am interested in meeting with you to discuss how my combination of accounting savvy and computer systems know-how can help you make the transition.

For the past three years, I have worked as chief bookkeeper for Banc One—Madison. I have also extensively studied multi-tasking spread sheets in Excel and Lotus. This combination could be invaluable in consolidating your information and setting a framework for the future.

Although I know your time is valuable, I would appreciate a few minutes to discuss how my qualifications could assist your immediate and long-term needs. I will call you on August 15th to arrange a meeting. In the meantime, if you'd like to get in touch with me, please call at 555-2386.

NILS EBERT
Marketing Associate

Three weeks after Nils had sent a cover letter and resume to Drummond Associates, he hadn't had a reply. Nils had already called and left several messages and wrote this letter to get the company to respond to his request for an interview.

Dear Ms. Brown:

I can imagine how crowded your schedule must be with your regular duties, and now you must be inundated with job applications; therefore, I am taking the liberty of following up on my previous correspondence. I feel that I am particularly well suited for the new position as Marketing Associate at Drummond.

I believe that my proven ability to work with senior managers and garner their support for sales efforts could benefit you right away.

During my six years at Gram Inc., I coordinated activities between various sales programs, senior management and outside vendors to develop in-store merchandising aids, including floor displays, shelf systems and signage to market a wide array of health care products. I feel my combination of skills and on-the-job experience ideally match your needs.

Because I think that once we meet you will quickly understand how I could best be of use to Drummond, I will call you on June 15th to set up a meeting. I can be reached at 201-555-7878 if you have any questions.

SARINA COLEMAN
Stockbroker

Sarina Coleman had scheduled a telephone interview with a prestigious Wall Street firm. To set the stage, she wrote a pre-interview letter.

Dear Ms. Waters:

I am looking forward to talking with you on March first at 2:00 P.M. I will be awaiting your call at 617-555-6896 as scheduled.

In the meantime, I am reviewing the material about your programs and noting questions we can go over during our telephone meeting. I will also share with you some ideas I have about marketing variable annuities that should apply to your new financial product line. If you are satisfied with our conversation on the phone, we can set up a face-to-face meeting.

I have marked up parts of the enclosed resume to emphasize my solid experience in both brokerage and product design work. It is this combination of skills that I believe will be most valuable to Blair as you continue to seek new financial markets.

I await your call and the opportunity it presents.

RICHARD ELLSWORTH
Travel Consultant

Richard had retired from manufacturing and was looking for a "fun" job. Since he had always been an avid traveler, he thought he might be able to offer his knowledge and hands-on experience to a local agency. Richard applied for a position as a travel consultant and had an interview. Because he wanted to make sure that the details of the interview stayed fresh in the employer's mind, he sent him a letter to recap.

Dear Mr. Ottomanelli:

Thank you for breaking bread with me yesterday. It was such a relief to find such a venerable peer—I thought everyone in your agency would be under 40!

Now that we have talked about the job in more detail, I am more convinced than ever that my extensive globe-trotting and my enthusiasm for travel would make me a good addition to your staff.

Since my main interest in this job is to be involved in the travel industry, I don't have any unusual starting salary requirements. As long as responsibilities and challenges are available, the salary you presented suits me just fine.

I hope to hear from you in the next few days and hope to get together soon. I have many ideas on how to get the job off the ground quickly and profitably.

ELLEN SPRINGER
Paralegal

After five years of being at home with her family, Ellen was ready to re-enter the workforce. Prior to having children, Ellen worked as a paralegal. She applied for several paralegal jobs and was granted an interview at one firm. Because she knew she was up against several other applicants, Ellen felt she needed a boost. So she sent her potential employer a competitive follow-up letter by messenger.

Dear Mr. Mitchell:

Thanks for meeting me this morning about the opening for a paralegal.

I know there is competition for this position, and I want to underscore how I think my qualities will help your firm.

My recent time away from paralegal work has given me real excitement and interest, and you can count on me to bring to the job a real commitment and the ability to work well under pressure. As a homemaker with a young child (lots of time pressures!) I've had to learn new ways to schedule my time and set priorities.

My community work taught me to pay attention to the needs of customers and colleagues and to work with others as a team. I brought my professional skills up to date with a recent refresher class at Ulster Community College

Please call me with any questions. I'd like to stay in touch and hope you don't mind if I check back with you soon to arrange another meeting.

BETH ROSS
Project Manager

After Beth was interviewed for a project manager post, she learned that the project she was to head was put on hold indefinitely. Beth decided that her only alternative, if she wanted a position with the company, was to offer her services as a part-time consultant so that she could establish a relationship with the firm and be the most likely candidate when a full-time position opened up.

Dear Mr. Kincaid:

You were very kind in your positive feedback about my work. Thanks for the compliments.

I was looking forward to working at Miramar and am very sorry that the position is on hold for a couple of months, because it is possible that I won't be available then.

As an alternative, I would like to offer you my services as a part-time consultant to help lay the groundwork for this project and others like it so that when funding is allocated you can move quickly and efficiently.

While you wouldn't be obligated to hire me when the job does open up, you will have had a good chance to see my skills in action.

Thanks again for your time. I will call you next week to discuss my idea for consulting possibilities.

PETE STOKES
Engineer

Pete, an engineer with twenty years experience, was granted interviews by several companies. When the first offer came in, it was not the one that Pete wanted. He was still hopeful that another company he'd interviewed with wanted to hire him, but with a wife and kids to support, he didn't have the luxury of turning down the first offer. Pete needed to send the first company a delaying letter and then follow up with a phone call to clarify his points.

Dear Ms. Stasi:

Thanks for the offer for the position of documentation engineer at Quasi Corporation. You have a great organization and I would be happy to join you.

While I know I can do a super job for you, I have a few remaining questions. I am working on another project for two more weeks, but once I've finished, I'd very much like to meet with you to talk again about the position at Quasi.

Thanks for your interest. I'll phone you in the next few days to review this delay.

RHONDA JACKSON
Merchandising Manager

Rhonda was an experienced merchandiser who lost her job with Federated Stores when they went through a major downsizing. She had been sending resumes by the dozens with little response and no interviews. She finally decided that the "mass market" approach in job searching was not to her advantage. This cover letter represents her strategy to pinpoint her cover letters to specific companies one at a time.

Dear Mr. Appleby:

The Limited has long been a primary example of merchandising at its best. Your ability to integrate consumer feedback into the design and manufacturing process is, of course, well known and your results, legendary.

As an experienced merchandiser, I have stayed in touch with your methods and those of other leaders in the field. Today, I know that you must be very interested in the merchandising now being pioneered by QVC, PRODIGY, and others who are using media and computers to connect directly to customers. This is an arena I have been following closely and one in which I could provide significant knowledge. This letter is to request a meeting with you to discuss a possible position with your merchandising department.

As you will see from the enclosed resume, in my work with Federated I was directly involved in their catalogue business and helped put together their first video catalogues. Although this project was later canceled due, I believe, to miscalculating who the audience was, I gained great insight into what I call "techno merchandising." I would like to share this experience with The Limited.

I will be coming to Columbus in two weeks, and would like to take advantage of this trip to meet with you. I will call to see how we can arrange this.

JANE BEAMER

Art Director

Jane got the job she wanted and then it was time to negotiate a salary. She accepted the job and opened the way toward salary negotiation in one letter.

Dear Ms. Allen:

I am very gratified by being offered the position of City Manager.

Before I accept, however, I would like to talk to you further about the compensation package. Given the scope of the job and the current parallels in the industry, I think that a profit sharing adjustment of some magnitude would be appropriate. This would serve both of us, and I will explain my position when we next meet.

I will call on Monday to see if we can get together right away to go over this one last item.

SALVATORE ALBANO
Baker

Salvatore had graduated from a culinary institute and was in the midst of the interviewing process when he received his first offer. He was not, however, ready to make a decision, feeling (a) that he had not had a chance to see what else was available, and (b) that the bakery offering him a job was too commercial for his interest. Since he did not have other offers in hand, Salvatore turned down the job in a way that would keep doors open.

Dear Mr. Smart:

Your offer is extremely attractive, for it gives me a chance to expand my knowledge of commercial baking. However, at this early stage of my job search, I am still exploring the opportunities in my field.

Right now, I am committed to baking bread on a smaller, more specialized scale. But in the future I might want to turn to commercial baking. When that time comes, I hope to talk to you again.

Thank you for having such confidence in me.

ABOUT THE AUTHORS

TOM JACKSON, chairman of Equinox Corporation and founder of the Career Development Team, Inc., is one of the nation's leading authorities on human resourcefulness, high performance, and the way people deal with their work lives and careers. He is the author of several best-selling books on career development and the job search. More than one hundred thousand people worldwide have participated in his innovative programs.

BILL BUCKINGHAM, president of Equinox Interactive, has over two decades of experience working with dislocated workers and career changers. He has designed and published several innovative and award-winning software programs on career and job search management that have been used by individuals, universities, and corporations throughout North America and Europe.